Migration Myste

Contents

Written by Inbali Iserles

Collins

1 Taking flight

It is late summer, and the evenings are beginning to grow shorter. There is a slight chill in the air. An osprey looks across woodlands and a nearby lake.

The osprey was born here, in the high trees, only three months ago. She has never left her woodland home. Now this large, clever bird of prey spreads her wings. She is about to fly more than 5,000 kilometres over land and sea. She will travel alone, without a **satnav** or map.

How can she tell that it's time to leave? How does she know where to go?

Let us investigate the mysteries of migration ...

an osprey prepares
to take flight

3

What is migration?

Every year, when summer turns to autumn in the **Northern Hemisphere**, millions of birds fly to warmer **climates**. As winter turns to spring, they fly back – often to find **mates** and raise chicks. Some **species** travel on their own. Others move in large groups called "flocks".

cranes in Hula Nature Reserve, Israel, one of the main migratory routes between Europe and Africa

In this book, we will begin to unravel the mysteries of migration.

- Why do birds migrate at a particular time of year?
  - Why do some birds migrate – but not all?
    - What stops birds from crashing into each other?
      - Why do flocks of birds form arrow shapes in the sky?
      - Do all birds fly south?
      - And – most baffling of all – how do migrating birds know where to go?

migrating knot birds in the East of England

2 Survival

Why do some birds migrate? How are their habitats likely to change in winter? What might be scarce in the cold months?

It's all about survival – the ability to stay alive in a world full of danger.

a cedar waxwing

Survival

Finding shelter, warmth, food or a mate can mean the difference between life and death.

barnacle geese

Why did birds begin to migrate?

Some birds started to fly further than others in search of food, to find mates or to nest in safety. Those birds were more likely to survive long enough to raise chicks. In turn, their chicks were more likely to migrate and survive.

What began as short trips became longer journeys over time, probably because of changes in climate.

Scientists believe that birds changed their behaviour in response to the ice age, travelling further and further to find food.

The last ice age ended about 12,000 years ago. The ice sheets across Europe and North America began to shrink. Flowers bloomed in spring, bringing huge numbers of insects like bees and butterflies. This was good news for insect-eating birds.

Ice ages

FACT

Over millions of years, the climate on Earth has had warmer and colder periods. Sometimes – like now – the weather is mostly **mild**. At other times, sheets of ice covered large parts of Europe and North America. These cold periods are known as ice ages.

As summer moved into autumn, the **conditions** became tougher. Some birds returned to the warmth of Africa or South America before winter arrived. Other birds stayed.

a bald eagle in winter

3 Why don't all birds migrate?

Why do some birds migrate while others don't?

Scientists looked at a large number of birds to find the answer.

The scientists discovered that it comes down to **energy**.

Save energy?

Option 1

Stay at home and save energy for the cold winter months ahead.

Option 2

Put all of your energy into a long journey south, knowing that life will be easier when you get there.

Short-eared owls from Scandinavia and Canada geese travel south for winter.

So why not stay in hot countries? Why do migrating birds make the long and dangerous journey every year?

Spring in Europe and North America is warm and wet. There is blossom on the trees, and the flowers are in bloom. These are perfect conditions for huge numbers of insects, which many birds eat. Spring and summer days are longer in the north than in the **tropics**. This gives birds more time to find food for their hungry chicks.

In the tropics, there isn't the same "insect boom" and there are more **predators** – animals that hunt the birds.

Different species have found their own ways of surviving their **environments**.

- **Most birds from the far north migrate.**
  Winters are incredibly cold towards
  the Arctic. Birds that stayed
  home would use more
  energy keeping warm
  through winter,
  and they wouldn't
  have enough
  food to survive.

an Arctic tern

Longest migration

The Arctic tern has the longest
migration of any animal.
It flies from the Arctic to
the Antarctic and back – that's
a 35,000 kilometre round trip!

- **In tropical rainforests like the Amazon, more birds stay put.** The environment does not change much through the seasons. The rainforest is always warm, and is home to insects and other food.

- **In countries like Great Britain, about half of the birds migrate.** Birds that travel south for winter are mostly the ones that eat insects, because insects are hard to find in winter. For example, nightingales migrate while many seed-eating finches stay all year.

The tropical bird of paradise does not migrate.

4 Flying solo

Remember the osprey who left home for the first time? Why did she choose to migrate in autumn, not in summer or winter?

The young osprey is following the path of her **ancestors**. Her **instinct** to fly in autumn is as natural to her as the ability to fish.

If this instinct wasn't there, the osprey might leave too early, before she had built up enough strength to survive the flight. She might leave late, making the journey too cold and tiring. She might not go at all and starve during winter.

The young osprey left at the right time. She is a survivor.

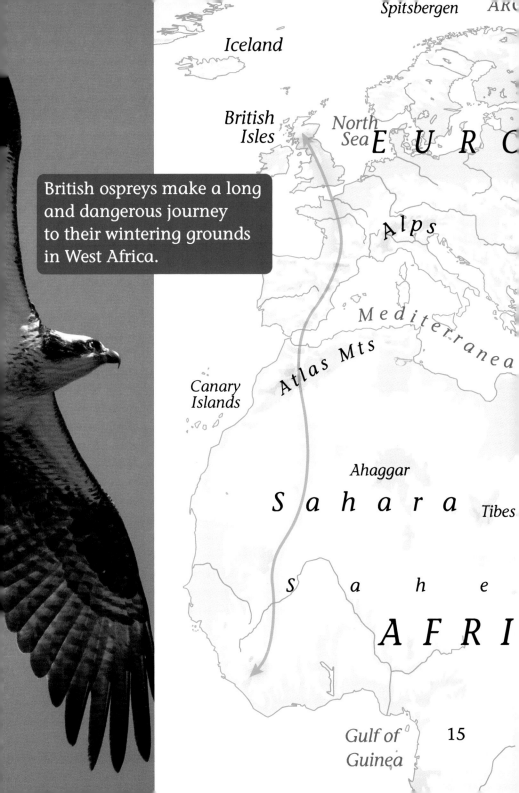

Spitsbergen

ARC

Iceland

British
Isles

North
Sea

E U R O

British ospreys make a long
and dangerous journey
to their wintering grounds
in West Africa.

Alps

Mediterranea

Atlas Mts

Canary
Islands

Ahaggar

S a h a r a

Tibes

S a h e

A F R I

Gulf of
Guinea

15

Ospreys do not live in flocks.
They migrate to Africa
on their own.

What do you think
the dangers are of migrating?

The young osprey needs to eat
plenty of food before setting off,
so she has enough energy for the trip.
She will have to cross the Mediterranean
Sea on her way to Africa. She may be
able to stop along the European coastline
to fish or rest, but not once she crosses
the open water.

The osprey runs the risk of being blown
off course. If she ends up lost over the wide sea,
she may not have the strength to find land.

The osprey has a special way
of saving energy during the long
flight. Like other large birds,
she can spread her wings over
currents of hot air called "thermals".

Riding the thermals

Thermals lift the birds without the need for flapping of wings. Once high enough in the sky, the birds soar with the thermals. Flapping is hard work, especially with huge wings! Riding the thermals is an excellent way to save energy.

FACT

an osprey riding the thermals

17

5 Birds of a feather

Like most birds of prey, adult ospreys live alone unless they are raising chicks. It makes sense that they migrate alone. But what about birds that live in flocks?

a **colony** of Cape gannets, South Africa

Safety in numbers

Some species of birds move around in flocks. Many watchful eyes are better at spotting predators, like cats or foxes. And while a predator is likely to notice a large number of birds, with so many birds in one place, a single member of the flock is unlikely to be caught.

Birds may also nest together in colonies to be near food, such as fish.

Social birds, like white storks and European bee-eaters, migrate in flocks. There can be hundreds of birds in these mass migrations. How do they manage not to crash into each other?

European bee-eaters and white storks

Have you ever tried to catch a fly in your hand? It's almost impossible! Birds, like flies, are incredibly quick at changing direction.

a flock of budgies in Western Australia

Rules of flight

Experiments on budgies showed that they keep on the right when they fly around objects. Scientists also discovered that the budgies flew at different heights. This stopped them bumping into each other in mid-air.

6 Formation migration

Some large birds migrate in highly organised flocks, like geese. Have you seen geese fly through the air in a "V" **formation**? Why do they make this shape?

Snow geese migrating from Canada in a "V" shape. Fighter pilots use the same shape.

- **Energy** – remember that migration is all about making the most of your energy. Each goose in the "V" flies a little higher than the one in front. This stops too much wind hitting them and makes flying easier. Geese take it in turns to lead, dropping behind when they get tired.

- **Keeping track** – the "V" shape allows the geese to keep track of each other so that none of the flock is left behind. This makes the journey safer for everyone. Fighter pilots use the "V" shape for the same reason!

How do we know that birds save energy by flying in a "V" shape? It's thanks to large birds called pelicans.

Scientists found that pelicans flying at the back of the "V" had slower heart rates than those at the front. The birds at the back didn't need to flap their wings as much.

Pelicans and northern bald ibises fly in formation to save energy.

Heart rate

Your "heart rate" is the number of times your heart beats per minute. If you exercise, your heart works harder and beats faster to get **oxygen** to your body. If you relax, your heart rate is slower.

The way birds flap
their wings matters
when they fly
in formation.

Flying to the beat

Scientists looked closely
at flights of the northern
bald ibis. These birds are
large, with very long wings.
The scientists found that
the birds beat their wings
at the right time to catch
the wind created by the bird
in front. This means they
save energy and can travel
longer distances without
needing to rest.

25

7 Flying south

People often talk about birds "flying south for winter". But couldn't we also say that southern birds fly north for summer?

Unlike most birds, the northern lapwing flies east to west.

ATLAN

OCEA

North or south?

Scientists looked at 800 species of songbird to understand where they originally came from. They found that, long ago, migration mostly started with birds searching for warmer climates. Many tropical birds that do not migrate had migrating ancestors. These birds became comfortable in the tropics and decided to stay!

Azores

Canary

Cape Verde

While most migration does happen north to south, or south to north, this is not always true. For example, the northern lapwing migrates east to west from Russia to Western Europe.

Spitsbergen ARCTIC OCEAN

eland

tish
sles

North
Sea

E U R O P E

Ural Mts

Alps

Black Sea

Caspiar

Mediterranean Sea

Atlas Mts

Zagros Mt

Ahaggar

Sahara Tibesti

Arabian

Peninsul

Red Sea

S a h e l

27

AFRICA Ethiopian
Highlands

8 The highs and lows of migration

Fly south, fly west … or don't fly at all?

Adélie penguins migrating on land

Migration without flight

Antarctic penguins can't fly, but some swim north at the start of the cold season, or make difficult migrations over ice. Large, flightless birds like ostriches are also known to walk long distances for the climate.

FACT

Not all migration covers huge distances. Some birds don't travel far but migrate up or down – from mountains to valleys. This is known as "**vertical** migration". For example, skylarks move from hilly areas to lowlands at different seasons.

Skylarks migrate downhill to the lowlands.

Disappearing habitats

FACT

Sadly, skylarks – like many other birds – are struggling to survive. Skylarks once lived happily on farms, but as farming methods have changed, it is harder for the birds to find seeds to eat.

Moult migrants

Some birds migrate in order to lose their feathers.
These birds are known as "moult migrants".

What is moulting?

Every year, birds lose their
old feathers so that they
can grow new ones. This is called
"moulting". The same word is
used to describe loss of fur on
animals like cats and dogs.

Shelducks lose all their flight feathers when they moult. They can't fly until their new feathers come through. This can be dangerous as it makes it harder for them to escape predators. So the shelducks migrate to moult.

Shelducks are moult migrants.

Every year in late summer, British shelducks fly to the island of Heligoland in the North Sea. They stay on the island while they moult, safe from predators. They fly home to the mainland once their feathers have grown.

9 The bird's compass

How do migrating birds know where to go?

Scientists believe that birds
have a "compass" inside
their bodies, telling them
where to go. This compass uses
a force called "magnetism".

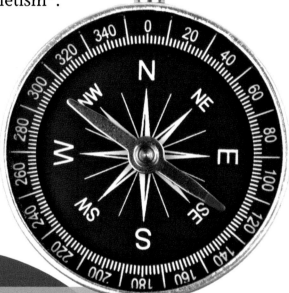

What is magnetism?

The force that makes a magnet
work is called "magnetism", and
it can work over large distances.
It's like an invisible magnet tugging
things closer, or pushing them away.

Magnetism across planet Earth is what
makes a compass point north.
Humans can't see this magnetism,
but we now believe that birds
can – and that they use it to
work out which way to fly!

Experiments on robins and zebra finches show
they can actually see magnetism!

What senses help a bird to migrate?

Eyes – make a "map" of the world around them using the Sun and stars, and landmarks like mountains. It is thought that birds can also see Earth's magnetism.

Ears – tiny amounts of metal in birds' ears allow them to feel Earth's magnetism, helping them understand north, south, east and west – just like a compass.

Beak – makes a "map of smells" that helps birds **pinpoint** their exact location.

These senses work together to tell the bird where to go.

10 Climate change

What does climate change mean for migrating birds?

Birds have followed the same migration routes for years. The ice ages are likely to have changed the way that birds behave, but this did not happen overnight.

The global temperature on Earth is rising.

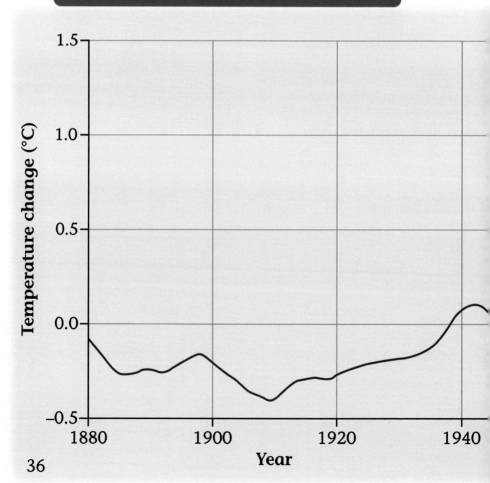

Humans use lots of energy for things like cars, factories and heating. At the same time, we have cut down forests to build farms and cities. This is changing the climate around the world, leading to consequences like:

- ice melting faster at the North and South Poles

- sea levels rising

- plants flowering earlier, or later, than they used to.

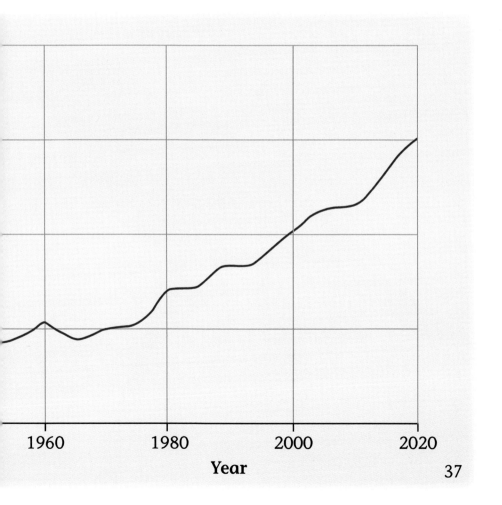

1960   1980   2000   2020

Year

Climate change is a problem for most animals, but it is particularly hard on migratory birds. These birds need conditions to be right at each part of the year: where they nest in spring and summer, where they go in winter and the dangerous journey between the two.

Most European migrant birds are expected to fly further on their travels because of climate change.

In future, European bee-eaters may have to fly 1,000 kilometres further.

Efforts are being made to protect the routes taken by migrating birds.

a great snipe

Fastest flyer

The great snipe has the fastest migration speed. It flies 6,760 kilometres non-stop from Sweden to Africa. Its average speed is an incredible 97 kilometres an hour!

FACT

11 Flying home

We have read about the wonders of migration, and some of the challenges that birds are facing. How can we understand more about birds, and what can we do to help them?

- Keep a notebook to write down the birds you see out of your window. Do they change over the year?

- If you have a garden, balcony or a community garden, make it a wildlife **haven**! Can you plant wildflowers to attract bees and butterflies?

- Use bird feeders to help hungry garden birds and make sure they are regularly cleaned to stop diseases from spreading.

- Join an **eco council** at your school to help protect the environment. If your school doesn't have an eco council, start one!

Together, we can be a voice for nature.

Make your garden a wildlife haven.

Do you remember the young osprey who left her woodland home on her first migration? She has spent three years in Senegal, on the west coast of Africa. She rested, fished and warmed her feathers in the African sunshine. Now she is fully grown, and ready to have chicks of her own.
Her instinct tells her it is time to leave.

The young osprey rides the thermals.

The young osprey takes to the air once more.
She flies north, looping around the Sahara desert.
She rides the thermals with her huge wings.
After an exhausting, four-week journey, she locates her woodland home. The osprey will rest, but not for too long. It is time to find a mate and build a nest.

Soon, the osprey will lay eggs in a tree not far from the one where she was born. And so the circle of life continues.

the osprey with her chicks

Glossary

ancestors members of an animal's family that lived before it

climates the sorts of weather places normally have

colony group

conditions what it is like in a place, for example, the weather

eco council a group of people who work together to protect nature

energy the ability to move and do things

environments places

formation organised in a particular pattern

haven a place which is safe

instinct a natural feeling to behave in a particular way

mates partners for raising chicks or cubs

mild not too hot or cold

Northern Hemisphere the top half of the world

oxygen an invisible gas that's in the air that we breathe

pinpoint find exactly

predators animals that hunt other animals

satnav an electronic device that helps you to find where you are going

species a type of animal, e.g. for birds, a blackbird or robin

tropics the area around the middle part of the globe where it is warm and wet

vertical something that points or stands straight up

Index

Why do some birds migrate?

Birds migrate for some or all of these reasons.

For food: bee-eaters eat insects that are scarce in northern winters.

For warmth: Arctic terns escape the freezing winters of the North Pole.

To mate: European ospreys fly back to their nesting grounds to mate and raise chicks.

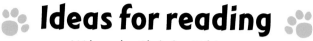

Ideas for reading
Written by Christine Whitney
Primary Literacy Consultant

Reading objectives:
- be introduced to non-fiction books that are structured in different ways
- listen to, discuss and express views about non-fiction
- retrieve and record information from non-fiction
- discuss and clarify the meanings of words

Spoken language objectives:
- participate in discussion
- speculate, hypothesise, imagine and explore ideas through talk
- ask relevant questions

Curriculum links: Science: Living things and their habitats; Writing: Write for different purposes

Word count: 3009

Interest words: environments, species, climate, conditions, formation

Resources: paper, pencils and crayons, access to the internet

Build a context for reading
- Ask children to name as many *species* of birds as they can. Check understanding of *species*. Do they see any birds in the school grounds or near their homes?
- Show the book cover to them and read the title, *Migration Mysteries*. Ask for a volunteer to explain the meaning of the word *migration* and another to explain why the word *mysteries* is used.
- Ask the group *Why do birds fly south for the winter?*

Understand and apply reading strategies
- Read together up to the end of Chapter 1. Support children as they read the questions on page 5 and suggest answers to them.
- Continue to read to the end of Chapter 3, page 13. Ask children to summarise why *some birds migrate while others don't*.
- Ask children to read Chapter 4 independently. Challenge them to explain the meaning of the word *thermals* and why riding the thermals is *an excellent way to save energy.*